E-Commerce Business Social Media Marketing

Simple Steps to Start your E-Commerce Brand/Company through Facebook and Instagram Marketing.

———————————

GoldInk Books

BEFORE YOU START READING, DOWNLOAD YOUR FREE DIGITAL ASSETS!

Be sure to visit the URL below on your computer or mobile device to access the free digital asset files that are included with your purchase of this book.

These digital assets will complement the material in the book and are referenced throughout the text.

DOWNLOAD YOURS HERE:

www.GoldInkBooks.com

Table of Contents

Introduction

- Are you confused about what kind of marketing strategy you should invest in?

- Do you have a limited marketing budget and want to spend it wisely, as you have already wasted a lot of money for the sake of promoting your business?

If answers to the above questions are YES, and you have been facing failures in promoting your business despite spending a large budget on its promotion, then I have found a sensible way to spend your limited marketing budget. In return, you will be able to gain impressive marketing strategies through social media. Small companies may utilize social media marketing as one of the most flexible and cost-effective methods to reach their target audience and increase sales over time. That is why 97 percent of marketers use social media to communicate with their target consumers.

This book is a must-read for all the brand owners who have recently established their businesses. Let me tell you the story of one of my friends. He established his business at the end of the year 2019. He spent a lot of money on many things such as printed advertisements and ads etc. You all know that Covid 19 hit the economy in 2020. So, his business failed miserably because he did not use E-commerce Business strategies. My friend never considered marketing his business through social media platforms. I advised him about Ecommerce business and marketing through social media. He used my advice, and his business got successful.

To promote your business effectively through digital marketing and social media, you first need to learn about E-Commerce Business. Through the E-Commerce business, product sellers and network operators may quickly improve sales and income. Online retailing is a widely used sales technique all around the globe. E-Commerce is an excellent method to transform your business from a conventional cinderblock shop to a cutting-edge, well-known brand. It provides excellent goods 24 hours a day, online customer service, and blogs through social networks. People nowadays really do not have a moment to go purchasing.

Conversely, an increasing number of people prefer online shopping for the goods they want anyway. If your business can provide this for your clients, there is no reason why you should not appeal to a wider variety of audiences looking for simple and accessible knowledge. Not only have E-Commerce tools improved throughout time, but there are also more of them available than ever before. Thanks to everything from selling platforms to marketing automation and SEO tools, even bootstrappers can get up and run without breaking the bank. In chapter two of this book, you will learn how to build your own E-Commerce Business.

Now the question arises how you will market your brand through an E-Commerce business? The answer is that you can easily do its marketing through social media platforms such as Facebook, Instagram, Twitter, TikTok, LinkedIn and, Snapchat, and many more. However, I have only written about Facebook and Instagram in detail in chapters three and four of this book.

Now, the next question arises for most of the readers: why should they believe anything I write in this book? Am I right about this question? I guess I am. Well, let me tell you about myself. I am a renowned online marketing strategist and have published multiple marketing books. I had unprecedented access to several former and current Amazon employees and Bezos family members who have provided me with in-depth information on how Bezos transformed his company to make it what it is today. Reading it will provide you with a great perspective and is perfect for new digital entrepreneurs looking to get started out on the right foot. I am writing this book because I have been in this field for the past 20 years and have helped many popular entrepreneurs to start their own E-Commerce businesses from scratch. So, let's start the journey of learning E-Commerce through social Media Marketing.

Chapter 1: Basic Understanding of E-Commerce Business

In E-Commerce, product sellers and network operators may easily improve sales and income by using internet commerce. Online retailing is a widely used sales technique all around the globe. There is a simple fact that many people buy things online. If your goods are not available online, you are losing out. Due to the epidemic, more individuals are now avoiding going to a physical shop, which has increased E-Commerce business growth.

The first-ever online transaction took place on August 11, 1994, when a guy sold a CD by the group Sting to a friend via his website Net Market, an American sales chain network. This is the first instance of a customer buying shares of a company via the internet, or "E-Commerce" as it is currently known.

Since then, E-Commerce has progressed to make it simpler to find and buy goods through online merchants and platforms. Individual freelancers, small companies, and big organizations have benefited from e-commerce, allowing them to offer their products and services on a larger scale than conventional offline shopping.

The most basic definition of E-Commerce is the "exchange of goods and services via the internet". It is essentially the same as purchasing anything online or doing some internet shopping. If you are one of the millions of Amazon customers, you are certainly acquainted with e-commerce from a customer's perspective.

It is typically a business-to-business (B2B) or a business-to-consumer (B2C) transaction (B2C). The vendor places an internet ad for his or her goods or services. The product is discovered and purchased online by a client (another company or a straight consumer). The buyer receives digital goods straight away. Physical items are delivered to the buyer's designated location.

1.1 How Does It Work?

The fundamentals of online business are similar to those of an offline/retail shop. The whole E-Commerce process may be split into three key elements or labor operations on a larger scale:

Receiving Orders

This is the initial stage, in which consumers submit orders through an E-Commerce platform (website or official website), and the vendor records them.

Details on Order Processing

The second stage involves processing and completing all of the order's information. It is now ready to be sent.

Shipping

The delivery procedure is completed at the last stage. All logistical components play a major role in this phase to guarantee timely delivery to the client.

If you get the fundamentals right and run your E-Commerce company correctly, you will make a lot of money. Always keep in mind that a popular tech shop relies on good business strategy and execution.

1.2 Types of Product Business Models

For innumerable purposes, E-Commerce has become a viable business strategy. One of the major reasons is that it has provided many companies with a low-cost or no-cost alternative. E-Commerce has provided a low-cost alternative to existing companies since it does not need a physical shop. As shown below, there are five different business models.

Customer to Customer (C2C)

Consumers may freely exchange products and services with one another in an online environment under the C2C paradigm. Craigslist and eBay are two of the more well-known instances since they were the first ones to use this approach.

C2C companies earn money by charging service fees. Motivated consumers and vendors gain a lot from such an E-Commerce model, as they help it develop while making money. However, it is not to suggest that running a C2C company is simple. You will have to deal with a lot of competition since this model has been around for a long time. Moreover, to lure the most customers, you will need to pay special attention to tech upkeep and quality assurance; the last thing you need is a public relations disaster.

Business to Customer (B2C)

This is the most well-known and well-established kind of E-Commerce business. Customers purchase goods and services immediately from B2C companies. Wall Street stock shops exemplify this business model. A B2C transaction may be anything you purchase at an online shop, practically anything. When opposed to B2B, B2C companies do not need to expend as much on promotion since most of the services and products they provide are of lower value.

Consider this: it is quite simple for you to determine whether or not you would like to order a new headset. However, because of the shorter sales cycle, B2C companies will have to put in more effort to retain strong client connections. Given the increasing importance of advertising in brand promotion, it is prudent to elicit favorable reactions from customers.

Business to Business (B2B)

B2B is a kind of business-to-business exchange that usually involves producers and distributors or resellers. One of the most well-known instances is Amazon, which provides companies with a customer-accessible network.

They engage with greater products and often repeat purchases. B2 B transactions have a longer sales cycle. This kind of E-Commerce business thrives with proper planning and good communication.

Payment processing employees at a firm are responsible for such contacts, maintaining professional commercial connections.B2B entrepreneurs are focusing on enhancing their E-Commerce shops and focusing on specialized markets. There are a variety of specialized companies available, such as CRM software and eLearning graphics.

Lair Superfood is another case of B2B E-Commerce. They cater to both consumers and companies (B2C) (B2B). You need a strong server leadership way to maintain sellers' transaction processing, warehouse and inventory control, etc. A B2B E-Commerce site usually needs a lot of money and a larger expenditure than a B2C E-Commerce website.

Business to Business to Customer (B2B2C)

This E-Commerce business strategy is amusing since it is a hybrid of B2B and B2C rather than a separate entity. In its simplest form, B2B2C is a partnership between two companies that establish beneficial trade services or product distribution networks.

To elaborate on this model, Business A, which creates a product, collaborates with Business B, which offers a special package – an E-Commerce portal. Business B has access to many users and therefore offers Business A large number of leads and sales, allowing Business A's goods to reach a large number of people. What comes to mind when you think about Business B? Yes, Amazon has done it again. Moreover, Business A may be any other Amazon seller, such as Apple or Samsung.

Peer to Peer (P2P)

A peer-to-peer (P2P) service is a decentralized platform that allows customers to communicate openly with each other without the need for an intermediary. This allows them to do financial business with each other.

There is a higher chance that the service provider would not deliver or the customer would not pay if there is no third party present. The danger is that more transaction costs will be replaced. As a result, P2P platforms provide services to their users to guarantee the quality of transactions, such as processing payments, data on producers and consumers, and quality control.

Online marketplaces such as trading cryptocurrency, document sharing, such as Napster, are all instances of P2P services.

1.3 Different E-Commerce Platforms

Every E-Commerce company needs an online shop, an internet landing page where consumers can browse, learn about, and buy their goods. As we will see below, E-Commerce companies have a variety of choices when it comes to the online marketplaces, they use to sell their goods online:

Shopify

Shopify's E-Commerce platform enables shop keepers to offer a wide range of goods and services. It is a deeply featured E-Commerce system. It came with an "out of the package and prepared to use" interface with several unique and helpful features.

Users may arrange and display goods as they like, monitor and fulfil orders, and accept money online through PayPal, credit, or debit cards using the system's configurable themes.

It is an easy-to-use platform that makes it simple to establish your E-Commerce shop and quickly get your company fully operational. The procedure of creating your shop is quite simple. After joining the program, you may choose from over a few multiple internet shop layouts and modify them to your taste, eliminating the need to hire a developer or have any previous design experience. The website designs available are aesthetically stunning and should be optimized to increase consumer conversions.

It is an internet application. It also provides hosting services on a server infrastructure designed and optimized for E-Commerce. As a company owner, this means that you will have one less overhead expense to monitor since you will not have to host your website somewhere. Another excellent feature is that Shopify also provides offline options, such as chip and swipe Reader equipment, that can simply be connected with your ongoing systems. This is especially helpful if you currently have a physical shop.

BigCommerce

BigCommerce has been one of the top E-Commerce suppliers, hosting over 4000 online shops and even some of the industry's biggest names. It is a fantastic choice for people who do not have any technical skills or coding expertise but need a system with many built-in capabilities.

BigCommerce bills itself as a web E-Commerce site for rapidly expanding businesses, promising more traffic, better conversion rates, and unmatched efficiency. Order fulfilment, analytics, digital payment integration, newsletters, and discount supply are just a few of the services listed. It also offers a 15-day free trial that gives you complete access to all of the system's features—the only downside is that, although you may build up your complete shop throughout that time, your clients will not be able to purchase anything until you change your price plan.

In contrast to other platforms, the major disadvantage is the absence of free shop themes. While it only provides seven free templates for company owners to choose from on some platforms, it is also concerned about data security. They utilize SSL to secure all of their client data and have edge hacking group equipment firewalls. BigCommerce is a fantastic platform to operate your internet retailers such as Amazon since it has a good reputation in the past and provides excellent customer assistance via comprehensive manuals, videos, and other resources.

WooCommerce

WooCommerce is the most adaptable E-Commerce platform available, which may explain why it is so famous among artists and E-Commerce programmers. They can be as innovative as they want with the platform's capabilities. It is an open and free e-commerce platform based on WordPress. This is fascinating because it is the ideal blend of business and information, with a large scale for personalization. It can operate with the greatest range of extensions on the internet while giving a feeling of familiarity to people who are already acquainted with the web application of WordPress, which is remarkable.

When you use WooCommerce, WordPress is the framework that allows you to create your shop's website. Although the core connector is free to use, you may expand its features and functions by adding other plug-ins. Although it is not the only plug-in for turning a Web application into an E-Commerce shop, it is by far the most popular. It means that there is a wealth of information and assistance available to assist you in getting your store up and operating.

Squarespace

It is a solution for those who value the visual and style aspect of their online store's user experience and design above all else. While it is somewhat "lighter" in terms of functionality, this does not detract from its overall impact. The system handles all mechanical tangents like hosting, names, and infrastructure, allowing you to concentrate on other areas of your company without performing any real work.

There is not much of a training course regarding utilizing the platform since the UI is aesthetically appealing while still being very simple. Squarespace is one of the finest options for building a beautiful website that reflects your brand image and appeals to your target audience if you do not have any technical skills. There are thousands of designs to select from, all of which can be easily modified to meet your specific requirements and simply integrate online payment interfaces.

The fact that you may utilize several layouts on the same site and have a customizable product layout instead of the usually categorized views is one of the things that sets Squarespace unique. The platform has a Blogging Module, which is useful for web analytics and website metrics and stats. They offer metric data for your shop. Squarespace has a search engine design and instantly optimizes your website for mobile devices, which is essential considering how many people buy on their smartphones or tablets.

The restrictions Squarespace has when it comes to growing your company are one of the reasons it does not score higher on our list. Because it only offers one payment method and no connections with sites like Amazon, it loses out. Squarespace is a fantastic choice for boutique entrepreneurs catering to a specialized market or shop owners working on a small scale. However, those wanting to expand on a large scale and quickly should look elsewhere.

BigCartel

BigCartel is an E-Commerce site geared for artists and designers. It has all of the features of a standard E-Commerce shop, but it is so easy to use that you can set up your whole business and have it up and operating in minutes. To keep it basic and simple, the functionalities of this platform are severely restricted. It is essential to remember that this medium is only appropriate for a few types of innovative brand concepts. This system may even be irritating to an experienced E-Commerce expert owing to its "over-simplicity."

BigCartel bills itself as an artist-centric platform, and its attitude is reflected in the way its infrastructure is built up and the site's design. It is all about purchasing this product and delivering it to the consumer as quickly and painlessly as possible. The platform focuses largely on its intuitiveness to market itself to prospective shop owners, which is why you would not find any complicated UX design or features. It is also ideal for any entrepreneur who is new to selling online and wants to keep their company modest by selling between 1–20 items on their online shop. Despite its straightforward approach, the platform offers a few key features, like order and inventory monitoring and control, no service charges, Facebook and Google Analytics integration, and an SEO framework.

It is also so focused on aesthetics and style, one of its biggest assets assists you with your marketing. They have some excellent marketing features built-in, such as time-limited offers and pre-orders. You would not be able to build your store exactly how you want it, and important features like implementations with payment options platforms, a search engine feature, and decreased additional product features will be lost as well.

1.4 Importance of E-Commerce in Business World

If you are still on the fence about starting an E-Commerce shop, here are the reasons why it is so essential for your company and how you may profit from going online this year.

It Expands your Brand

E-Commerce is an excellent method to transform your business from a typical cinderblock shop to a leading-edge, renowned brand. Your company can become the destination of your products and the particular home of your company, enabling you to fully broaden your various definitions without needing to worry about relocating places or worrying about being not ready to broaden your company.

It is more Accessible

An online business is open 24 hours a day, seven days a week, allowing your consumers to shop whenever they want, regardless of their schedule. People nowadays really do not have a moment to go shopping. Subsequently, an increasing number of people prefer online shopping for the goods they want anyway. If your business can provide this for your clients, there is no reason why you should not appeal to a wider variety of audiences looking for simple and accessible knowledge.

It Extends your Reach

Many people around the world can see your website at any moment, which means that a broader audience has a lot more options. When you consider the number of people you can contact via a website vs a high street shop or promotional campaign, there is no explanation you must not consider putting your company online if you want to expand your reach.

It Gives You Possibilities for Advertisement

Your webpage is one of the most powerful marketing tools. You can not only use SEO when constructing your site to increase the chances of your company being found on web pages, but a variety of other sales tactics, such as pay-per-click adverts, social marketing, and lead generation, can all involve website traffic.

It is More Adaptable

As your company develops, you will most likely want to expand your product line and target market and improve your company to meet client needs and consumer demand. An E-Commerce site allows you to extend your company as needed, enabling you to add more products, more payment methods, and even expand where you ship to, without worrying about relocating to a bigger location like you would with a physical retail shop.

E-Commerce provides a wide range of services to businesses, from marketing to expanding product lines to boosting revenue. With a well-designed and improved website, you can succeed and provide your clients with a comfortable facility that can enhance the company.

1.5 Pros and Cons of E-Commerce Business

E-commerce has changed the contemporary marketplace in recent years, and you do not have to be a business expert to notice it. While it is common, selling products or services online has its own set of benefits and drawbacks.

It enables companies to increase their client base while eliminating the need for physical shops. Their sites provide a significant benefit to both consumers and businesses that are not situated in large metropolitan areas, in addition to removing the risk of lengthy lineups. Rent, utilities, maintenance, and other expenses connected with physical shops may all be reduced. Without employing staff to keep an eye on the shop and safeguard the goods, your e-commerce store may effectively operate 24 hours a day, seven days a week. Digital goods may be sold online for very little money.

Consumers may buy items right away, thanks to e-commerce. E-commerce companies frequently find it simpler to communicate with their consumers. Sending both automatic and personalized emails is easy since the e-commerce merchant collects contact information through email.

Finally, e-commerce enables your firm to monitor logistics, which is critical for a successful e-commerce operation.

Everything becoming digital makes it simpler to gather data and calculate statistics automatically. While understanding what is selling well may be beneficial, the low-volume items allow you to take more chances.

While it may seem that moving from a physical location to an online shop would solve all of your company's issues, there are some drawbacks to doing so. Many customers still prefer the human touch and connections that may be established in a physical store. Customers looking for specialist goods may find this particularly useful, since they may wish to contact an expert about the best product for their requirements. When it comes to online purchasing, security and credit card theft are major concerns. Every time a user enters personal information into a website, they are exposed to identity theft and other risks. Consumers are left empty-handed if buying is about immediate pleasure. They are often forced to choose between paying extra for expedited delivery or waiting several days for the goods to arrive.

Chapter 2: Building Your Own E-Commerce Business

Businesses all around the globe must move faster than they have in the past. Brands are being pushed to adopt a new way of doing business due to more competitors, customers, and the changing economy. This chapter gives an in-depth insight into the steps involved in establishing a new E-Commerce business.

2.1 Plan Your Foundation

Some people buy online for the sake of convenience, while others do it out of need. It is impossible to deny that internet shopping has become a way of life for many people. The demand is only expected to increase. Knowing your desire to establish an E-Commerce company is not enough. You must have a clear concept of the kind of E-Commerce company you wish to start. You can create a business plan, but having a clear idea of where you want to go is crucial if you want to succeed.

If you establish an E-Commerce branch of an established company, your present business model will point you in the right direction. These models have been discussed in the previous chapter.

Decide on a Niche

A niche is a segment of a broader market that is specifically targeted. This term may define both an item or brand and the target audience for that product or service. Organic beard wax for guys with curly hair, for example, is a special product. Guys with curly beards who are health-conscious are a subgroup of the broader market of men who use grooming products.

Do not make the costly error of attempting to create a company that caters to a large audience. To prevent overpaying and disappointing all of your prospective clients, make sure you design your company to suit the requirements of a particular niche. If you start your company with a specific product or service intended for a specific set of individuals, you are more likely to succeed.

Perform Market Research

It is time to do market research once you have defined your company strategy. Online company ideas abound, but you must first determine a viable market for your planned venture. The first and most crucial step is to begin your research. Do not make decisions based on a hunch. Any internet company is a long-term investment. There is no one-size-fits-all company model that works for all of us. The list goes on and on, with service-based businesses, software, digital product sales, and physical goods only scratching the surface.

Print on demand is a good option if you want to make money without handling your goods or spending a lot of money upfront.

If you have your warehouse full of goods, you will need to spend more money upfront and utilize a wholesaling or warehousing model. Do you have a business idea for the ideal product or a particular item you want to sell under your brand? Investigate white labelling and production options.

2.2 Check Legal Matters

Creating a business format for your company may be daunting for new entrepreneurs. Make sure you do not make a hasty choice. Spend some time instead learning about your preferences. Evaluate which structure is best for your company, and each form may help you achieve your professional and personal objectives now – and in the later, as your company develops. The structures are as follows:

A single proprietorship is the most straightforward kind of company. A sole proprietorship implies that the earnings and obligations of the company are entirely the responsibility of one individual.

A partnership is a shared responsibility for a company between two or more individuals who are personally liable.

A Limited Company is a business form that allows owners, partners, or shareholders to restrict their liability while maintaining a partnership's tax and flexibility advantages. A corporation is a legal body that exists independently of its owners. It implies that the company may own property, be held responsible, pay taxes, and engage in transactions.

You will need licenses and permits to lawfully run your company after you have decided on your lawful business model. Make sure you enroll with the government and the Internal Revenue Service (IRS). Your company structure determines the paperwork you will require and where you will have to register. The SBA website has a complete set of paperwork for each kind of business. On the same website, you may discover government tax requirements.

You may require national, state, or municipal licenses and permissions to function in certain instances. You may search the SBA's website for state regulations by state and company type. Also, check with your town to determine if any local licensing or state regulations exist.

One would also need to obtain a tax ID from the IRS, known as an employer identification number. It is not necessary if you are a single proprietor with no workers. However, you should get an employer identification number to keep your individual and commercial taxes distinct and ensure that you can easily employ when the moment arises to grow your company. If you are unsure whether you will need an employer identification number to operate your company, the IRS offers a handy guideline.

2.3 Create a Brand Identity

Every business has its brand image. Even if you have made a natural intentional branding choice or not, this is valid for your business. That is why it is critical to make deliberate and regular branding decisions. Your company's brand represents how others think about and view it. This encompasses your company's stated purpose and values, as well as the goods and services you offer and how you market them. This entire brand image will serve as a beacon for your company, leading it back to its roots in terms of identity and values.

Name of the Company

Your company name can measure almost every element of your company. It is how people will recognize and recall you. As a result, it is critical to pick a name that properly reflects your business. Otherwise, your E-Commerce shop would go undetected by your intended audience, attracting incorrect (non-buying) leads. Your company name will define your internet name. As a result, your company name would become your internet address, which consumers will use to locate you. You must pick a company name that reflects your brand and is accessible on the internet.

Logo

A company logo is more than simply a picture. It also functions as a brand image, grabs new customers, and seems to be reliable. A well-designed corporate logo effectively communicates to consumers that the firm is competent, reputable, and offers high-quality products and services. As a result, the company's growth is accelerated.

How to Create a Business Logo?

First and foremost, it is essential to link the style of a corporate logo to the nature of the firm. Decide on a color scheme as well. It is crucial in the growth of a brand. We should attempt to differentiate our logo from our competitors in terms of color and style. To develop a stunning logo, you may use Adobe, Vector illustrations, and Layout applications. Many apps are accessible in both free and premium editions for non-technical users. They may use this to make a nice logo for their company.

What is the Best Way to Utilize a Business Logo for Branding?

We utilize logos to link the site to a particular brand. We use the logo as a business symbol on workplace wall hangings, office boards, banners, visitor cards, and ID cards.

2.4 Develop a Product or Service

You have the required context to create a product or service that can flourish after grasping the strategy of your company, market, and particular niche. If you want to sell pre-existing items, start by looking into different possibilities and then compiling a list of goods that suit your business.

When it comes to the sale of goods, be selective. You should offer goods that attract your intended audience while also reflecting your purpose and the values of the company. Providing consistent goods with your business and the perfect consumer will demonstrate that you "understand" them. It will also encourage customer loyalty and encourage customers to return. You presumably have a reasonably clear concept of what you would like your item to be if you are clear about its label and how you will produce it. However, before approaching a producer, you will need to finalize the specifics and product design. Consumers' problems are solved with the finest goods. As you collaborate with your design engineer, make it your primary goal to solve that issue.

A service is abstract and difficult to show via the internet. This makes selling services more difficult. Begin by jotting out a list of general services you would want to provide. Then, before posting your proposal online, double-check every aspect. It begins with a thorough definition of your services and outputs so that you may provide your clients with the most comprehensive image possible. If you want your company to flourish, you must demonstrate prospective consumers.

2.5 Create your Online Market

When you eventually create your shop, you will need the design information you decided on at the previous stage. Your online store must also be suitable for the layout you choose.

Your E-Commerce company revolves around your website. It is where the digital road meets the tyres. Customers will learn about your company, examine your goods, and fill their virtual grocery cart and check out all in one location if you have served your time correctly. This is not enough to have a visually appealing website. To have an E-Commerce website accomplish all it requires to do, it needs to have some actual code guts behind all this. Follow the other given steps to create your online market.

Choose your Platform

There are dozens of E-Commerce online store platforms to choose from. It is not simple to select the best E-Commerce software. Factors like downloading speed, functionality, connectivity with multiple payment options, consistency with your company structure, your web development abilities, SEO-friendly features must all be considered carefully. Some of these platforms have been covered in the earlier chapter.

Several electronic systems offer free website designs that you may utilize. However, we suggest going with a system that allows you to create your distinctive look. Using a web design shared by hundreds of other small retailers is a guaranteed way of incorporating it. If you like your online shop to be noticed, it must have distinct visual brand recognition. Launching with a generic style that anybody can use makes attaining that objective an uphill fight.

Furthermore, layouts reduce your authority over your online shop, restricting your right to modify the style and look for branding purposes. Templates that say "what you will see is what you will get" are simple to use. They are, however, limiting and hard to expand.

Create a New Website Design

Your business name should serve as a source of creativity as the centerpiece of your visual identity. It is worth noting that your main objective is to have multiple approaches to purchase and choose design decisions that complement your visual identity.

Make your Product Descriptions

Item displays are something that every online shop has in similar, irrespective of design or platform. When you create engaging listings, your sales will soar, while not captivating listings will remain stagnant. All the most significant and poorest listings have three things in common: product names, descriptions, and photos. This is how you implement them that determines whether you succeed or fail.

- **Listing**

To your prospective consumers, your listing names distinguish your goods. The more detailed your listing name is the more information about your goods a buyer may acquire at a single look. Before consumers even go through, you can demonstrate what sets your brand different and why they could not live without it. Your listing names will increase purchases if you use a dynamic method that can emphasize your goods' most delicate features.

- **Images of the Products**

The highest sales tool is good product photos. Buying over the internet carries a higher level of risk than purchasing in person. You can inspect and handle an item in your own two hands at a shop. Consumers are unable to touch the goods they want to buy while shopping online. Great design photography may help to alleviate some of that fear. Take pictures with good lighting. Experiment to see what time of day provides the most excellent illumination for you. Keep in mind that these images must appeal to your intended audience. As a result, keep those consumers in mind while styling the photographs.

- **Descriptions of Products**

The last stage in producing a fantastic listing is to write a tremendous product description. This is your chance to convey your product's narrative. Include all of the specific things that make your goods attractive. Assist prospective consumers in visualizing how the item could fit into something and enhance their lives. Most often, people make purchasing choices based on their emotions rather than their brains. So, instead of just listing characteristics, create an attractive image with your words to get more significant outcomes.

Finally, check over the statements written by your top components. Follow their well-crafted content at any cost. However, you may receive suggestions for what kind of material to include or how to arrange it.

2.6 Market your website

E-Commerce marketing is the process of driving visitors to your online retailer, turning that visitor into paying consumers, and keeping those customers after they have bought the item. A well-thought-out business plan may help you raise brand recognition, improve customer retention, and boost online sales. You may use E-Commerce advertising strategies to advertise your online shop as a whole rather than to generate more excellent sales for particular items. A few fundamental things to attempt are listed below.

- **SEO Strategy**

It is a must-have feature for e-commerce companies. Your goods must rank higher than those of your competitors, and they must be displayed correctly so that prospective consumers can discover the things they require in the SERPs and engage on your site. E-Commerce objective functions, when done correctly, may help you rank higher and offer the most excellent answers to a user's query purpose. Improving E-Commerce sites may provide you with a steady stream of free and increased client traffic.

In reality, if an online store fails to convert a guest into a client, the time and money spent acquiring that person are wasted. When it comes to E-Commerce website optimization for sales, it is all about focusing on four distinct goals that are explained as follows:

1. Find the appropriate individuals for the job. Most E-Commerce companies would like to attract a limited number of genuine customers to their site instead of a large volume of visitors that consumes information but never converts.

2. The majority of transactions are not the product of a specific search. Instead, consumers usually make several inquiries during their purchasing process. It is a common misconception that visitors who have already visited your site will return as they prepare to buy an item.

3. The keyword searches vary as customers move down a sales process and remain on their purchasing experience. Buyers usually start with broad search terms to gather information and

then refine their search queries based on that information. The key to optimizing for SEO is predicting the details of this ultimate search engine.

4. Keyword research is at the heart of every successful E-Commerce SEO management plan. It is critical to make sure that you are addressing the correct keywords when it comes to SEO. Choosing the incorrect target term may hurt your views and send lesser visitors to your website.

- **Starting a Blog**

Blogging may be a powerful tool for a businessman or corporation to use to expand their E-Commerce store. Businesses with blogs often rank better in search engine results and get more visitors than otherwise. Furthermore, if you aim to grow your client area and enhance sales, you would not be disappointed with a blog.

A blog may serve as a basis for your company to share its experience and business knowledge with the rest of the world. When you establish yourself as a confident figure in your industry, you will have a better chance of persuading your readers to utilize your goods or services since they will remember your suggestion and site first if they need assistance in buying the product.

What else would your blog's primary goal be to bring in new consumers? Every time you post material, it must be engaging enough to entice your viewers to buy your goods or utilize your services. More significantly, it must assist in increasing the exposure of your site.

An excellent method to expand your E-Commerce company is to enlist the assistance of other companies. Recommendations from other businesses may help you develop new business connections that can benefit your own company. You may accomplish this by writing an article on complementary goods to your company or profiling some enterprises. You may also invite other companies to submit guest posts to your blog.

Connection marketing is becoming increasingly popular as a means of establishing a fast connection with the consumer. You may utilize a blog to publish crucial data, news items, or even advancements relating to your area of study, making it a fantastic venue and tool for customer loyalty. You can also utilize social media advertising to find out who your target customer is and then write blog articles just for them. Now that you know how important blogging is for growing your E-Commerce company, it is time to start posting.

- **Email Marketing**

Email marketing is a subset of internet marketing, which includes webpage, social networks, and blogging, among other things.

Newsletters containing business information and special offers for members are examples of email marketing. In the aftermath of a major catastrophe or a corporate crisis, marketing emails may attempt to convey a broad message on the firm's account. Email marketing, at its finest, enables companies to keep their consumers updated while also tailoring their marketing messages to their specific target. At its poorest, that kind of marketing may drive consumers away by regularly sending them unpleasant junk emails.

- **How Does It Work?**

Email marketing is simple to start up and monitor, allowing access to small companies. For example, you might provide a newspaper sign-up choice on your website. You may have exposure to a growing fan base as individuals join up. Customers may also sign up for the newsletter via your social media accounts. A daily letter is an easy and efficient method to keep your customers informed about new products, forthcoming activities, and promotional deals. Email marketing software also makes it very easy to send out automatic marketing offers to clients who have not bought the product in a while.

You may use email marketing to reach specific categories of consumers or even individuals. One method to accomplish this is to offer particular clients some special birthday discounts on goods or services. On their anniversaries, a restaurant, for example, could send an email to clients giving a discount on a meal. This kind of customization aids in developing and maintaining a client connection, which may lead to higher sales and customer satisfaction.

- **Advantages of Email Marketing**

There are many advantages of email marketing, but some are as under:

> **Low Prices**

One of the most apparent benefits of email marketing is that it is less expensive than traditional marketing methods. There are no expenses for printing or shipping, and no charges are given in return for visibility on a specific billboard, newspaper, or TV network. To organize, monitor, and analyze their communications, email marketers should probably invest in specialized software. Although there may be a minor expense associated with sending millions of messages at once, these costs are much lower than those associated with other traditional marketing methods.

➢ Reach Out to a Group of Interested People

Email marketing is one of the few media that customers specifically want. The majority of companies that use the site only send emails to people who have requested them. Because a company is just going after people already interested in their brand, selling prices may be considerably greater.

Of course, sending unwanted marketing emails is possible, but this will simply irritate customers and harm your brand's reputation. It is highly advised against using bought lists for email marketing; the benefits you will get from naturally building your list and gaining consumers will be much superior.

➤ Send Messages to Specific People

Most marketers would gladly pay to guarantee that their revenue would only go to those engaged in their brand. Email marketers may take one further step by delivering emails exclusively to subscribers who match specific criteria. If a business only has a public offer in particular parts of the nation, it is simple to set for mails to be delivered exclusively to those who live in those regions. If there is a deal on sporting items, only those that have expressed curiosity in athletics will get an email.

Brands that want to learn more about their users may use email list division to their advantage. According to studies, marketers who utilize this strategy have a higher connection as a consequence. The old spray and pray approach of delivering the same message to every member or client is no longer effective. The businesses that get the most outstanding results from email marketing divide their information and programs to guarantee that they deliver the most appropriate message to each person.

➢ Quite Simple to Use

To be effective with email marketing, you do not need a large staff or a lot of tech expertise. With sophisticated themes, videos, pictures, and logos, an email campaign may be made to stand out. Despite this, some of the most decisive victories use introductory modest text emails, implying that the essential aspect of an email is its information.

➢ Simple to Share

Members may easily share fantastic discounts and offer with their contacts by just pressing a link. There are not too many forms of marketing that are as readily disseminated as this. Members may soon become brand advocates dedicated to exposing your company to new markets. Brands are increasingly using this strategy, and content marketing is becoming a significant factor in internet sales in recent years.

➢ Immediate Effect

Due to the speed of email, a company may notice benefits within minutes after sending an email. A twenty-four-hour sale is an excellent email marketing strategy because it generates concern and persuades subscribers to act immediately. In the case of printed advertisements, businesses must usually have to wait for weeks for sales to flow in.

• Social Media Marketing

The adoption of social media portals to advertise your goods or services is known as social media marketing. The common individual spends three hours each day on social media apps, and 60 percent of social browsers use social media to do research online. It is an integral part of the marketing jigsaw that cannot be overlooked. From increasing brand recognition and site traffic to simply interacting with your consumers tangibly, social media marketing may help you accomplish various goals. All of this may lead to better converts and revenue, giving your initiatives a win-win situation.

Whenever it relates to social media marketing, most companies use one of two methods.

1. Organic Social Media Marketing

An organic social media approach focuses on non-paid methods of connecting out to the intended audience. When you post material to Facebook or Instagram, and it appears in your viewer's timeline, this is an illustration of organic reach since you did not charge for the exposure. Organic social media tactics often aim to raise brand recognition while also connecting and maintaining an audience.

2. Paid Social Media Marketing

In a nutshell, paid social media marketing, also known as compensation when you click, would be when you spend a network like Facebook or Instagram to show your ads to its customers.

Your advertisements will not be displayed to anybody to guarantee that you receive the highest profit on your ad investment. In most cases, social media advertisements will be displayed to a subset of people depending on a set of characteristics or similar groups. Paid advertisements, in essence, definitely achieve new people who may not be acquainted with your brand – which is why you spend on this extra publicity. Depending on the platform, paid advertisements may be shown in various forms, including text or picture, rotation, and even video or narrative commercials.

Part of your choice on which social media site to employ in your marketing plan will be based if you are a B2B (business-to-business) or B2C (business-to-consumer) company. Let us look at the most well-known social media sites and how you may utilize them to promote your company and objectives.

- **Facebook**

Facebook, the monarch of social media networks, is a must-have in anyone's online marketing toolkit, from small companies to retail behemoths to e-commerce sites. Facebook can be an excellent medium for generating traffic in both B2B and B2C sectors since it has over two billion members.

- **Instagram**

Instagram, which has over one billion members, seems to be another popular social media marketing tool. Instagram's ad spending is 25 percent greater than Facebook's and with good cause. Owing to tags and the exploration tab, it still has a lot of organic reaches.

Instagram is an excellent option among e-commerce advertisers and performs exceptionally well for companies targeting B2C markets. With over 90percent of Instagram users having at least one company and per day usage durations of 53 minutes, it means that businesses should be engaged on the site as well.

- **TikTok**

If you are already following social media advertising trends recently, you will know that it is now trending. However, before you turn your eyes and declare that the network is just for children and teenagers, think again. Keep in mind that it has over 1 billion active members worldwide and is rapidly one of the world's most significant social media networks. However, just 40 percent of its users are between the ages of 16 and 24, indicating that it may be as valuable for companies as for content providers.

TikTok is primarily a video-based network that is most known for its tag competitions, as well as lip-sync challenges. 15-second videos aim to keep viewers involved long enough for them to go over to your account for more and subscribe to you.

- **LinkedIn**

If your target audience is companies (B2B), LinkedIn is a site that should be at the top of your priority list. LinkedIn has stayed constant in the notion that users are there for one reason only: to do business. It is the only platform of its type, and it is all about connecting, learning, and growing, as well as sharing and finding employment possibilities.

- **Twitter**

From Silicon Valley tech firms to presidents and prime ministers, everyone is on Twitter these days. Moreover, with over 150 million daily active users, you should be, too. However, if you are wondering how Twitter might help your social media marketing plan, consider this:

40% of Twitter users are said to have bought something after viewing it on the network. Not everything on Twitter, however, must be a direct reaction. This platform may also help you raise brand recognition, get mentions, and drive visitors to your website.

In further chapters, marketing through Facebook and Instagram will be discussed in detail.

Chapter 3: E-Commerce Business Marketing through Facebook

Facebook began as a social network, but it has evolved into much more than a corporate marketing tool. Besides going digital, operating an e-commerce company in today's market necessitates several things. While Facebook's e-commerce promotion and marketing need a well-thought-out plan, it also offers a different chance to reach a wider audience with your goods. Facebook's 2020 statistics show that the world's most extensive social network has more than 2.6 billion monthly members.

 Facebook is the most extensively used social networking site on the internet today. Its vast number of users are regularly engaged with the internet platform, which implies that your new online store has a great deal of opportunity in this medium. Even though you would not wish to be too pushy with your initiatives, new company entrepreneurs must establish an internet presence, and Facebook is a great place to start.

3.1 How Facebook Works?

Users and companies may use Facebook to share data, photos, and videos and interact with one another. Users of Facebook can:

- Set up a profile.

- Add other people as 'friends,' share conversations with them, and see their profiles.

- Anyone over the age of 13 may become a Facebook member.

- You need to go to Facebook and enter your name and email address. Facebook may be accessed through a laptop, as well as a smartphone.

Facebook User Profiles, Groups and Pages

You must first join Facebook by providing a genuine email address and a real name to create an account. Facebook will help the process of creating your profile. Your profile is a one-paragraph description of whoever you are and what attracts you. It is essential to add a picture to your account. You may share with people, relatives, colleagues, and people that match your hobbies by creating a profile. You must establish a page if you wish to advertise your company.

There are also groups on Facebook. You may also engage Facebook groups based on similar hobbies and activities after you have created a profile.

You can also create pages on Facebook for the promotion of businesses. To interact with their followers, prominent people and entertainers show Facebook sites. The 'Create a Page' procedure on Facebook will walk you through creating a page by providing you with a range of inquiries about your company.

Facebook Advertising

You can pay to advertise or support a post that will display to the Facebook audience, who might very well be interested in your content if you have a Facebook account. If you want to publish an ad or a promoted post, Facebook's business page will walk you through a step-by-step procedure to figure out who your intended audience is and how to prioritize your ads.

3.2 Why Is Facebook Important for E-Commerce Business?

A Facebook profile may help your company in a variety of ways. A few of these advantages are comparable to owning a website, while others are exclusive to Facebook. The benefits mentioned below may result in higher sales and profitability for your company.

Facebook Marketing is a Low-Cost Approach

Advertising strategies that would cost hundreds of dollars on some other platforms may be done at a quarter of the price on Facebook. This makes it suitable for small to medium-sized companies on a tight advertising budget. Larger companies may also use Facebook to test marketing ideas and themes prior to investing in more significant initiatives.

Provide Basic Statistics

A Facebook page is a place where you may promote your company's name, address, and phone number, as well as a short description of your items and services. You may also speak about your employees, your company's background, or any other element of your company that is effective to entice other Facebook users.

Share Your Company's Photos and Videos

Facebook allows you to submit visual content from your company in addition to text. This may be an effective method to connect with consumers and prospective customers since it will enable them to view your item or brand without coming to your location.

Speak with Prospective Consumers

You may utilize Facebook to 'speak' to current and prospective clients by sending and receiving messages. However, do not use Facebook to advertise your goods or services unnecessarily. You will have a lot more success if you provide data about your company that other people will find helpful or intriguing. By establishing long connections with other users, you enhance your reputation and promote your company. A vet, for example, might provide pet-care advice timed to coincide with the occurrence of specific health problems. You should pay as much attention to what others are saying as you do to what you are saying. Observing what the majority thinks about your company, industry, item, or advertising campaign may offer helpful information.

Assist Customers

Customers may ask follow-up inquiries on your Facebook page, and your employees can respond. This is frequently more practical than having someone answer the phone, and it enables other readers to view common queries and solutions without needing to contact you one-on-one.

Advertising Targeted Things

Facebook can analyze all of the data that millions of people put into their accounts. You may pay to utilize this information to send targeted advertising to a particular group as the owner of a company page.

Promote Offers

Users may use Facebook Places to 'check in' on their mobile devices in a specific area so that their contacts can see their position on Facebook. Facebook Places also highlight popular spots near a user's check-in location.

Businesses may utilize Facebook Places to provide a list of local companies providing offers when a user checks in to an area, street, or business. Only pages in the category set up as a Company and Organization or a Local Business may add a location.

3.3 Facebook Marketing Strategies

You may always hire a good marketing firm to help you with Facebook marketing for your e-commerce company. However, you may try your hand at Facebook advertising with these basic suggestions in the beginning. Follow the given steps for Facebook Marketing.

Determine Whom You Want to Reach

If you want to advertise your goods or services, you must first determine who wants them. You need to know their age, where they live, what they do for a living, and why your good or service is beneficial to them. The Audience Analysis feature on Facebook allows you to go further into your prospective consumers to learn about their ethnicity, career, marital status, geography, dialect, Facebook use, and even past buying.

Make a Facebook Page for your Company

It is cheap and straightforward to set up a Facebook company page. At Facebook.com/business, establish a business page and select from various business categories, such as local company or location, unique selling proposition, and group. Complete in the blanks to tell everyone about your business. Then, much like with your own Facebook page, add additional pictures or a symbol, the main picture, and a biography picture.

That is the backbone of your webpage, after which you will add a short outline of your company and valuable facts for your prospective clients. Create a name that consumers may use to reach you through Messenger. After that, you may add to your profile, specify your region, and start writing your first post. You are now officially in business, at only on Fb.

Directly Sell your Goods on Facebook

You may sell your goods directly on Facebook to supplement your e-commerce shop. Create a store to your Facebook profile so that consumers can buy straight from you. Go to your Facebook Page's "Retail" button to access the Business Supervisor's "Offer on Page" section, which allows you to connect business accounts, specify delivery and refund options, and arrange payments.

Produce Visual Content

To ensure that your goods or services sell themselves, make sure your e-commerce design is polished and very visible. In addition to content and comments about your interests, use excellent photos and videos. Do not overlook Facebook Live presentations, which are actual video replays that may immediately link your business with prospective consumers. Replace your product pictures and videos frequently. Allow consumers and onlookers to take part in the creation and display of images and recordings.

Maintain a Regular Publishing Schedule

Posting valuable and engaging content is essential if you want to engage consumers and grow your markets, and you should stick to a timetable, so your public knows when you update your blog daily or several times a day.

Your audience's reaction will determine your publishing plan. Be ready to modify your messaging as needed, but always keep a strict publishing schedule and post during increased retention hours. Most merchants post on weekends because consumers have more spare time on weekends, but the ideal time varies depending on your company.

Make your Goods Promoted

While you do not have to make your consumers weary with a sales technique all of the time, there is nothing wrong with placing your goods and services in front of an eager audience to create attention and purchases, particularly if you are launching anything new.

Engage with your intended audience, and be sure to let them know about any in-store specials. If you offer sufficient value, your network will be receptive to know about your goods and services through sale prices posted on Facebook for business.

Interact with your Consumers

Your customers and followers will frequently submit material on social media, which you should share with your community. You may also advertise freebies and other free things to create excitement and serve as a propaganda effort. Add consumer comments to your ads: User reviews of goods are among the most popular articles.

Use Facebook Advertising and Pixels to Promote

Using Facebook advertising to promote your business is a sure-fire method to get people's attention. All you have to do is to create a Facebook Ads account and pay to have your content shared with specific audiences.

This puts your advertisements in front of potentially interested consumers, allowing you to meet your conversion objectives of turning lookers into purchases. Brand recognition, user engagement, app downloads, and shop visits are just a few of the possibilities available to marketers on Facebook.

Set up a pixel account regardless of what you decide to do. Set up a Facebook Pixel, which is a code snippet that you put on your website to remarket to the individuals who have previously visited your website, even if you do not intend to utilize Facebook advertising immediately. The pixel aids in the creation of specialized audiences for future ads: When you put it on your site, it gathers data and sets cookies, allowing you to monitor visitors as they engage with your site or advertisements.

Combine Shopify with Facebook

Shopify is a popular and simple-to-use e-commerce platform with excellent Facebook integration for building websites, tracking and shipping orders, and selling in person or social media.

Use Shopify to personalize your site with a 14-day free trial that allows you to establish a Shopify Facebook shop called a Facebook Shop by connecting your Shopify account to your Facebook account. To connect your Shopify shop to Facebook, go to the "Facebook Shop" section of the sales channel's menu, choose your Facebook page, and click your account. Facebook will evaluate your shop and notify you of its decision to approve it, or you may check the status of your Shopify store by logging in.

Running Facebook advertising, providing a referral program, and employing affiliates are all examples of Shopify. Members get a portion of recommended purchases. Controlling the customer process and experience is one of the most significant advantages of having a Shopify Facebook Store.

Your customers become your own when you sell on Shopify, allowing you to advertise to them afterwards.

Nowadays, running an e-commerce business is challenging. A strong marketing campaign, bolstered by well-thought-out Facebook outreach tools, advertising, and a customer-centric approach, will go above and beyond to help your online business thrive.

Chapter 4: E-Commerce Business Marketing through Instagram

Instagram social media marketing is a technique you can certainly explore. Instagram content marketing has enabled some businesses to double their revenue in a matter of days – it is that effective. Using Instagram influencer marketing, you may advertise your newest goods, gain new consumers, and connect directly with current ones. Instagram boasts engages users per month, which means there is a big audience to be gained.

New advertising platforms appear regularly, as do the techniques and methods for using them. People are exposed to more advertisements than ever before. It is more important than ever to stand out from the crowd. Interactions with marketing must be pleasant and not too salty. Influencer marketing allows you to communicate with your target consumers without coming off as pushy - an advertiser's dream.

You will discover important Instagram marketing methods in this chapter. These tactics may be used to increase shop sales and brand awareness.

4.1 Importance of the Algorithm

We will go through the variables that affect our content's rating. The Instagram algorithm is beneficial to advertisers. The Instagram algorithm takes into account a lot more. Interest, timeliness, relationship, frequency, following, and use are the six criteria that decide what you see on your Instagram feed.

Interest

The order in which pictures and videos appear in your feed will be determined by the probability of your interest, your connection with the person posting, and the post's timeliness. Instagram analyses your previous behavior to determine your level of interest. So, if you interact with a particular genre of material more often, Instagram may prioritize content from that genre in your feed. Even if posts with lower engagement are more beneficial to you, they may still show at the top of your feed.

Reliability

Timeliness is the next important factor in the Instagram algorithm. Instagram aims to offer you up-to-date and more valuable posts. The Instagram algorithm re-orders new posts during your current visit and your previous visit. If you check your Instagram account at 11 p.m. and then again at 9 a.m. the following day, Instagram will only sort the posts generated during your review.

Relationship

Instagram does not at all need you to miss crucial postings from your friends and relatives, like your friend's engagement announcement. As a result, material from your "best friends" is likely to appear higher in your stream. Instagram's algorithm analyses your past encounters to identify which profiles you connect with the most often to decide who your closest friends are. Profile search is a factor that the platform considers when prioritizing photos in your feed.

Frequency

When you open Instagram once a day, you will see the posts that Instagram's algorithm considers the most interesting for that day. If you open Instagram every hour, on the other hand, the app will try to show you the most relevant information you have not seen before.

Following

If you follow hundreds of Instagram profiles, the algorithm would have to go through even more material to determine what to display every time you enter the app. Those who follow many people are likely to see fewer from each account, while people who want to follow just a few chosen arrangements are expected to see much more of their friends or favorite profiles.

Instagram Usage

What the algorithm displays depend on whether a person browses Instagram in quick bursts or for extended periods. If a user likes brief Instagram visits, the algorithm guarantees that the most relevant posts appear first.

In contrast, users who prefer more extended browsing periods may access a more extensive library of new material.

Why is the Instagram Algorithm Beneficial?

When social media managers are pushed into the Instagram algorithm, they attempt to find out how to defeat it. There is usually a public uproar when social media companies shift away from a sequential feed. The switch to a prioritized feed in Instagram's algorithm is a win-win situation. The system uses machine learning to guarantee that consumers receive the most interesting material, resulting in better-focused audiences for commercial accounts. It is beneficial to you if you create engaging, relevant, and timely material.

4.2 Effective Steps for Instagram Marketing

Instagram is quickly becoming the most famous social media platform on the internet. For companies that aim to get through their social media marketing, an Instagram marketing plan is a must-have marketing tactic. E-Commerce business owners can turn their stores into sales machines if they play their cards correctly. In 2021, Instagram E-Commerce will be the way to go. All you have to do now is implement a bright Instagram marketing plan that will enable you to grow your online shop substantially.

Make your Instagram Profile Stand Out by Optimizing your Bio

Ensure that your profile is tailored to your company's needs and target market. The only purpose of your brand's Instagram page should be to tell the narrative of your company. Another essential element to consider is your Instagram bio. At the same time, the biography must be both engaging and instructive. It should be attractive enough to entice others to follow it.

By Labelling Your Location

Your company must be reachable both online as well as offline. That is where the location tag comes in handy to assist you in finding your exact address. The location tag informs people where you can be found, and it increases your visibility by making you more visible in Instagram inquiries when others are nearby.

Create an Instagram Feed that Reflects your Brand's Style

Creating an attractive profile may be challenging, but it is still a critical Instagram strategy in 2021, and companies should not overlook it. Because Instagram is mainly a visual platform, one of the first important things to know about Instagram marketing is that the quality of the materials and the harmony of the colors and styles utilized are essential. Product pictures play a huge role in online purchasing, and Instagram's graphical interface can amp up this power significantly. Add your brand's style and passion to the feeds. Play with your brand's look and add brand image. Most essential, be truthful and authentic.

Use Your Imagination When It Comes to Captions

The key to enticing consumers on Instagram is using creative and new captions, but regularly captioning your picture or video is difficult. We have found that captions of up to ten words boost interaction on Instagram for companies, mainly when used in conjunction with rotating posts.

Concentrate on the Intended Audience

To conduct Instagram marketing correctly, you must first determine what your product or brand appeals to your target demographic and then represent this in your Instagram feed. Do not skimp on your posts and messaging content, and utilize this platform to connect with your audience via discussions about shared values and goals.

Use Hashtags to your Advantage

On Instagram, hashtags are used to help people find the material they are searching for. You should carefully utilize hashtags so that more people may discover your articles when searching. Here are some tips to help you get the most out of your Instagram hashtags:

- In each post, use no more than 2-8 hashtags.

- Choose hashtags that are widely used and searched for.

- Include hashtags that are only relevant to your desired customers - the number of clicks will be lower, but the value will be higher.

- Create customized hashtags if you are running a campaign or want to promote a particular brand.

- Choose location-based hashtags to promote your business in a particular region.

Increase the Number of Carousel Posts

We have found that carousel posts on Instagram resulted in a higher impression rate, indicate that your Instagram marketing plan should prioritize this kind of content. Slide posts are an excellent method to highlight a product, a new brand feature, a team article, and so on. You may include up to 8 pictures or videos in a carousel post, so make sure you utilize them all to emphasize your brand's message.

Keep Track of your Most Popular Instagram Posts

Always look at the statistics to discover what type of Instagram posts your followers are most interested in. Returning to your advanced analytics and looking for links between your most popular articles is another simple method to figure out what your subscribers enjoy. On Instagram, engagement is king, so take the benefit of having a community that can correctly guide you.

Last but not least, think beyond the norm! Do not be afraid to attempt new ideas, but remember to keep your audience. All social media sites' newsfeed algorithms are constantly evolving. As a result, whatever succeeded last week is unlikely to work the following week. Check to see whether you are up to date.

4.3 Instagram Marketing Strategies

Your business will be able to reach a bigger audience if you use an efficient Instagram marketing approach. Instagram may assist you in generating high-quality leads. It enables you to successfully create a community of devoted followers with whom you can share your goods and solicit comments. Let's look at some Instagram marketing techniques that you may use to increase your E-Commerce sales using Instagram.

Make a Batch and Automate It

One of my favourite Instagram marketing strategies is this one. Customers are looking for genuineness. They like it when companies participate in their buyer's journey discussions. Creating material from scratch every day, on the other hand, is exhausting.

Product Labeling

You should tag goods because they provide a clear call to action. It makes the customer's buying procedure more accessible. Instagram enables businesses to tag goods in their posts in the same way that they can tag individuals.

Tagging is one of the most effective Instagram marketing strategies for companies looking to reach a larger audience. The procedure is straightforward, and you can turn your Instagram account into a sales channel in no time. The easy steps below will get you started.

Create a storage area on your company's Facebook page linked to Instagram, and fill it with your goods. Customers will be able to check out on your E-Commerce website rather than on Facebook if you choose this option. As a result, your inventory management system will always be current. Wait until your Instagram account notifies you that you may begin tagging items. Select the "tag a product" option when uploading a picture to view a list of all the goods you have posted to Facebook.

Hashtags Help You Save Time

Instagram hashtags have a lot of power. Each post may include up to 30 hashtags. They make your work available to a larger audience. It aids in the acquisition of new prospective consumers. Do relevant hashtag research regularly to save time? After that, please make a list of hashtags you wish to use and keep it. If you regularly share product pictures, quotations, or lifestyle photos, for example, make a list of hashtags for each. At the time of publishing, add a few relevant hashtags to each post. Because trending hashtags often change, it is essential to keep your hashtag list up to date.

Always keep the user experience in mind while planning your Instagram hashtag strategy. Using Instagram to find new consumers takes effort and patience, but it is well worth it. Look for hashtags related to your goods so you can interact with consumers who share your interests.

Engagement Is the Crucial Factor

Spend some time commenting and following your target demographic on social media. This will allow you to develop naturally over time, with remarkable results. Others are more likely to visit your profile if you comment on their postings. Likes are cheap and plentiful. Engaging with your fans in a meaningful manner, on the other hand, attracts more significant attention. When you interact with your target audience, they are more likely to reciprocate likes and perhaps follow you.

It is not in your best interest to buy likes or followers. It may seem to be a fast cure, but it may harm your brand in the long term. Instagram does not disclose the rationale for censoring material when they announce an algorithm update. It is easy to spot accounts with a high number of followers but little interaction. Instagram has a reasonable possibility of shadow-banning your account and limiting your reach.

Analytics Should Be Considered

The best Instagram marketing plans usually involve a comprehensive analysis of statistics. The metrics in the app offer you valuable information. This information may be used to boost engagement. You can check when your Instagram followers are most active by going to the audience tab. Plan your future articles around these hours to get the most bang for your buck.

Keep an eye on the pictures with the most likes. It will offer your insight into what your target audience is most interested in. You may utilize this knowledge to improve engagement by posting more of what they desire.

Instagram's appeal is that it does not require significant expenditure. You can quickly boost your Instagram E-Commerce sales. Because Instagram users love buying, use the Instagram above marketing strategies for companies as soon as possible. Also, keep track of your progress. You should have enough data on the sales you made through Instagram within a month.

Conclusion

There is no dispute while saying the significance of E-Commerce. It has become necessary for retail companies to be accessible and open to consumers from all over the world, with no fixed period for buying goods. At this moment, there is no way of knowing whether or not the store is open. The business, as they say, never sleeps, and electronic commerce is all about assisting companies in maintaining and growing their income streams while also developing through time. The most important debate that businesses should be having right now is which kind of E-Commerce path to take. We can assist whether you wish to fly solo with a custom-built E-Commerce shop or use a pre-existing E-Commerce platform.

Customers are already searching for companies like yours on social media platforms. If you want your business to succeed on social media, you must understand Facebook and Instagram marketing.

Facebook is a must-have in anyone's online marketing toolkit, from small companies to retail behemoths to e-commerce sites. Facebook can be an excellent medium for generating traffic in both B2B and B2C sectors since it has over two billion members. Instagram is an excellent option among e-commerce advertisers and performs exceptionally well for companies targeting B2C markets.

I have developed this book, *E-Commerce Business through Social Media Marketing,* from personal and professional knowledge and experience in an effort to help you understand your situation and fix it. If my book has been able to achieve that goal, I am beyond happy for you. Please leave a review on Amazon.